# HAIL! THE CRIMSON
# AND THE BLUE!

*Hail! the Crimson and the Blue!*

*Hear the Chapel bells implore us,*
*Turn our thoughts to LMU.*
*Sing this song in joyful chorus*
*Hail! the Crimson and the Blue!*
*Here together we develop*
*Life of the heart, the soul, the mind*
*Men and Women, all for others*
*Knowledge, Justice intertwined.*

*For one hundred years you've heard us*
*Lions cheering on for you.*
*Roars throughout the world do echo*
*Still we find our home in you.*
*You have made us, loved us, and taught us*
*Values we will not discount*
*May it ring throughout the ages:*
*Hail! Loyola Marymount!*

*See the Tower — all admire! —*
*Keep her brilliant light in view.*
*Beacon on the Bluff inspire*
*All we can and ought to do.*
*May our mission ne'er be forgotten*
*Praise be the name of LMU*
*Hail to thee our Alma Mater!*
*Hail! the Crimson and the Blue!*

**NEW ALMA MATER COMMISSIONED FOR THE CENTENNIAL**
WORDS BY KELLY YOUNGER '94 AND RACHEL VAN HOUTEN '03

# CONTENTS

# LOOKING FORWARD

BY DAVID W. BURCHAM, 15th PRESIDENT

Thank you for joining us in commemorating 100 years of Loyola Marymount University. Our yearlong centennial is one of the most vibrant celebrations in the history of the university and brings the LMU community together like never before.

Beginning in 1911 as Los Angeles College, we have grown and evolved, undergoing a number of changes in name, location and structure, but always sharing common threads that weave their way through our history and bind us. These include our heritage as a Jesuit and Marymount institution, a commitment to academic excellence, our distinct sense of community, and a unique ability to inspire lives of leadership, service and purpose.

The theme of our centennial celebration is "LMU at 100: Learn. Lead. Serve." As we honor our past and look to the future as a preeminent Catholic university, this theme expresses our Ignatian roots and continued commitment to our mission of the encouragement of learning, education of the whole person, and the service of faith and promotion of justice. We also celebrate a century in Los Angeles, a thriving, historically-rich city that serves as the ultimate classroom for preparing students to become responsible citizens and shapers of the world.

I invite you to peruse this book to learn more about LMU's history, see how LMU has been marking its centennial and enjoy a few gems from our rich photographic archives. I also encourage you to continue visiting the centennial website (100.lmu.edu) as we will be adding new features and opportunities for you to participate in the festivities between now and May 2012.

It is a great honor and privilege to serve as LMU's president as the university marks its centennial. But it is you — our students, alumni, faculty, staff, parents, donors and friends — who have made LMU the outstanding university it is today and who will carry it into its next 100 years. Join me in celebrating this remarkable place, its steadfast mission and most importantly, the people who make us LMU.

Loyola University
Ground Breaking
May 20 – 1928
Crowd dispersing

# Imagining The Next 100

*The 2011–2012 Bellarmine Forum celebrates
our heritage while looking forward.*

THE BELLARMINE FORUM Each year, the Bellarmine Forum ignites conversation about the most profound questions of human existence. Through theme-based symposia, roundtables and other social events, the forum has explored the depths of such pivotal topics as vulnerability, immigration and the environment.

The Bellarmine Forum is traditionally a weeklong event. But this year is different. In honor of LMU's centennial, the forum has been expanded to cover the entire 2011–2012 school year — a sort of Bellarmine Blowout, if you will.

This year's theme, "Ignatian Imagination in the World: The Future of Education, Faith and Justice," heeds the university's centennial call to "Learn. Lead. Serve." by asking how we can re-create our faith to meet the dynamic needs of today's globalized world. Inspired by Adolfo Nicolás, S.J., Superior General of the Society of Jesus, and his charge to Ignatian higher education, the forum will revisit the values, charisms and continuing works of the three founding orders, and explore how best to carry their spirit into our next 100 years.

Throughout this special centennial year, alumni, students, staff, faculty, religious, colleagues, benefactors, regents, trustees and members of Loyola Marymount's far-flung community will be invited to consider Superior General Nicolás' charge. In addition, the Sisters of St. Joseph of Orange and the Religious of the Sacred Heart of Mary will challenge the community to consider compassionate responses to critical needs.

From symposia, roundtables and student presentations to performing arts, exhibits, author series and the indispensible pub night, this celebratory yearlong Bellarmine Forum promises to captivate, enrich and help lead Loyola Marymount University into the future, while never losing sight of its values of encouraging learning, educating the whole person and serving faith and promoting justice.

"What kind of universities, with what emphases and what directions, would we run, if we were re-founding the Society of Jesus in today's world?...I think every generation has to re-create the faith, they have to re-create the journey, they have to re-create the institutions. This is not only a good desire. If we lose the ability to re-create, we have lost the spirit."

**ADOLFO NICOLÁS, S.J.,
SUPERIOR GENERAL OF
THE SOCIETY OF JESUS**

**PAST BELLARMINE FORUMS**

2002
Globalization and Ethics

2003
The Color of God

2004
Violence: An Interdisciplinary Investigation Into the Human Condition

2005
Just Community: For All

2006
Environmental Responsibility: Earth to You. Do Something Now

2007
I|M|Migration

2008
Religion. Identity. Life. Convivencia?

2009
Vulnerability: Windows Into the Human Condition

2010
Imagining Equality: Women's Art and Activism

## 2011–2012 BELLARMINE FORUM

JESUIT (S.J.) SYMPOSIUM This inaugural conference focuses on Jesuit rhetoric as it examines ways in which the history of early Jesuit rhetorical education may speak to today's educational challenges and civic duties. The next two years will focus on the Jesuit philosophical and theological traditions respectively.

**CONFERENCE ON JESUIT HIGHER EDUCATION: RHETORIC, PHILOSOPHY, AND THEOLOGY**
Oct. 11–12, 2011
Von der Ahe Family Suite, William H. Hannon Library

RELIGIOUS OF THE SACRED HEART OF MARY (R.S.H.M.) SYMPOSIUM This symposium focuses on shaping "the future for a Humane, Just, Sustainable Globe" from the perspective of the Marymount tradition, the R.S.H.M. charism and the R.S.H.M. commitment to help create an alternative to the culture of domination and violence.

**TRANSCENDING BOUNDARIES: WORKING TOWARD A GLOBALIZATION OF SOLIDARITY AND HOPE ... SO THAT ALL MAY HAVE LIFE**
Jan. 19–21, 2012
Various locations, please consult Centennial Calendar

SISTERS OF ST. JOSEPH OF ORANGE (C.S.J.) SYMPOSIUM This symposium focuses on how the C.S.J.'s collaborative efforts seek to serve both Church and society. Discussions explore their mission to bridge the religious and social gaps that divide people, and to serve those most in need.

**COMPASSIONATE RESPONSE TO CRITICAL NEEDS: ENDEAVORS OF THE SISTERS OF ST. JOSEPH OF ORANGE**
March 29–31, 2012
Various locations, please consult Centennial Calendar

## 100 YEARS IN EIGHT EVENTS

The following eight events comprise our "Moving Forward, Looking Back: Imagining LMU's Next 100 Years" program, inspiring reflection, imagination and enthusiasm for another successful 100 years.

**STARTING THE CONVERSATION: Where is LMU headed?** This beach-party-themed event kicks off the 2011–2012 Bellarmine Forum as well as the "Moving Forward, Looking Back: Imagining LMU's Next 100 Years" events. Guests are invited to imagine LMU's next century.
Sept. 8, 2011
12:15–1:45 p.m., Amphitheatre and Lawton Plaza

**WHO WE ARE IS WHERE WE ARE: A Celebration of the Ignatian and Marymount Traditions** A chapel tour and shared stories from and about the Jesuits inspire discussion on the past, present and future of our Ignatian and Marymount traditions.
Sept. 30, 2011
Sacred Heart Chapel and Sculpture Garden
4–4:30 p.m. Tour, 4:30–5:30 p.m. Shared stories, or 5:30–6 p.m. Tour, 6–7 p.m. Shared stories

**100 YEARS OF SERVICE: LMU Gives Back** This outdoor event starts with an exuberant beach clean-up day and culminates in a celebration at the Loft.
Oct. 22, 2011
9 a.m.–12 p.m. Dockweiler State Beach
12:30–2 p.m. Reception at the Loft

**COMING HOME TO LMU: A Celebration of Our Student Athletes**
Faculty and staff are invited to a tailgate party to meet and celebrate our student athletes. Homecoming game to follow.
Jan. 28, 2012
6–7 p.m., Hannon Field

**CELEBRATING THE MARYMOUNT TRADITION OF THE VISUAL AND PERFORMING ARTS** The festival honors the merging of the Marymount tradition into the Loyola College family in the fine and performing arts.
Feb. 17, 2012
5:30–6:30 p.m.
Exhibits, Laband and Thomas P. Kelly Jr. Art Galleries

6:30–7:30 p.m.
Music and Dance, Murphy Recital Hall

7:45–8:30 p.m.
Film Screening, Mayer Theater
8:30 p.m.
Reception, Sound stage

**CONTEMPLATING LMU: A Tapestry of Spiritual Traditions** This guided tour from the heart of the campus to the edge of the bluff and back is led by LMU faculty, staff and spiritual leaders representing the myriad spiritual traditions embraced by the LMU community.
March 21, 2012
6–9 p.m. Roski Terrace, Tongva Memorial, Heliport, East Atrium

**THE HEART, THE BOOK AND THE GIFT: Shakespeare's First Folio at LMU and Shakespeare's Birthday Celebration**
The Marymount Institute of Faith, Culture and the Arts and the William H. Hannon Library present a braided reading with Jeff Dietrich, Lewis Hyde, Wole Soyinka and friends. Reception to follow.
April 23, 2012
Von der Ahe Family Suite, William H. Hannon Library

**CELEBRATING SHARED GOVERNANCE: 100 Years of Supporting Each Other**
As the centennial celebration nears conclusion, the Bellarmine Forum invites staff and faculty to enjoy an evening of friendship and food, honoring all of us who work hard to make LMU the excellent and transformative university that it is.
April 27, 2012

**ADDITIONAL NOTABLE SERIES AND EVENTS**

Archives and Special Collections Rotating Exhibits
All exhibits are located in the Terrance Mahan, S.J., Archives and Special Collections, William H. Hannon Library
Open weekdays, 8 a.m.–5 p.m.

Learn. Lead. Serve. University Archives celebrates 100 years of LMU Student Life
July 18–Sept. 25, 2011

Sustaining Splendor
Oct. 1–Dec. 22, 2011

100 Years of Service to LMU
January–March, 2012

The Heart, the Book and the Gift: Rare LMU Book Treasures
April–June, 2012

Pub Nights
First Wednesday of each month, first semester only, 2011, 5:30 p.m., Von der Ahe Family Suite, William H. Hannon Library

Alumni Authors Series
One Wednesday per month, second semester only, 2012, 6–7:30 p.m., Von der Ahe Family Suite, William H. Hannon Library

Jesuit Spirituality and High Finance: Can They Co-Exist in the 21st Century?
Oct. 18, 2011
12:15 p.m., Von der Ahe Family Suite, William H. Hannon Library

Los Angeles Interfaith Prayer Service
Oct. 23, 2011,
5 p.m. Liturgy, Sacred Heart Chapel
6 p.m. Reception, Sculpture Garden Von der Ahe Family Suite, William H. Hannon Library

Artists Speak:
Voices of Justice
Oct. 29, 2011
2:30 p.m., Murphy Recital Hall, Reception, Dunning Courtyard

Hidden Heroes:
Service to the World
Nov. 12, 2011
2pm, Murphy Recital Hall. Reception, Dunning Courtyard

Mission Day Roundtable:
"What Kind of Universities, With What Emphases and What Directions?"
Jan. 26, 2012
6 p.m. Reception
7–9 p.m. Roundtable, Ahmanson, UNH 1000

Loyola Law School's Second Annual Center for Restorative Justice Conference: Imagining the Future of a Justice that Restores in Los Angeles
Feb. 25, 2012
All day, LMU Campus (Various Venues)

**LMU FLOAT**
Decorating: Throughout
December 2011

Parade date:
Monday, Jan. 2, 2012

Time: 8 a.m. PST

Parade theme:
Just Imagine...

Location: Colorado Boulevard, Pasadena, Calif.

To purchase tickets in the LMU grandstand, sign up to help decorate or learn about the regional viewing receptions: **100.lmu.edu/roseparade**

**PAGE OPPOSITE** LMU's float nears the end of its construction. As the parade approaches, it will be up to LMU's students, faculty, staff, alumni and parents to decorate the float with a nearly incalculable number of flowers.

# THE CENTENNIAL IS TURNING UP ROSES

LMU will be a part of the Tournament of Roses Parade® for the first time in more than seven decades. On Jan. 2, 2012, the university will enter its own float in the 2012 Rose Parade®. The float will feature the William H. Hannon Library, Sacred Heart Chapel and a larger-than-life LMU lion when it rolls down Colorado Boulevard. President David W. Burcham and his wife, Christine, will join Robert Scholla, S.J., Mary Genino, R.S.H.M., and 12 other riders — students, alumni and friends of LMU — on a replicated LMU bluff, complete with its iconic LMU letters and hilltop benches. As the float makes its way along the parade route, the 30-foot bell tower will chime, celebratory fireworks will shoot skyward, and everyone will hear the lion's roar.

BUILDING UPON THE PAST In 1938, the Loyola University Band marched down the streets in Pasadena ahead of a float built by MGM Studios and entered by Culver City on behalf of the university. The float won first prize in its category, and Loyola received national attention as the first university band to march with a float entry. This year, LMU's float will herald our centennial celebration. Designed by Phoenix Decorating Co. and funded entirely by private donations, the float will be decorated by more than 1,700 members of the LMU community.

ADDING LMU'S PERSONAL TOUCH One of the great traditions of the Rose Parade® is a community's involvement in decorating its parade float. Alumni, parents, students, faculty, staff, friends and their families will put the finishing touches on LMU's float throughout December. During the week before the parade, volunteers will work around the clock to ensure LMU's float will be memorable.

CELEBRATING WITH LMU LMU has reserved two grandstands for the float's generous sponsors as well as students, faculty, staff, alumni, parents and friends of the university who purchase tickets. Additionally, alumni, parents and students who head home for winter break can gather at viewing receptions around the country to toast LMU's centennial as they watch the parade on TV. Jan. 2 promises to be a memorable day for LMU.

See more photos of the LMU float under construction at 100.lmu.edu/float

## PEOPLE POWERED

Nearly 1,000 Loyola
Marymount University
students, faculty and staff
became a white, blue
and crimson mosaic on
the green lawn of Sunken
Garden on Aug. 30, 2011,
to celebrate the school's
centennial and kick off
the new academic year by
forming a human "100."

The picture-perfect
celebration was accompa-
nied by cheers and chants
from the enthusiastic
crowd that donned T-shirts
in LMU's colors as they
waved pom-poms in front
of Sacred Heart Chapel.

The program made
the most of the first
Convocation Hour of the
year, when no classes are
scheduled and students
are free to assemble for
short programs, attend
the on-campus farmers
market or check out
campus clubs.

There was plenty of
singing and hugs among
returning classmates who
hadn't seen each other
since the spring, as well
as 100-year birthday cake
and tricolor cupcakes for
all. Iggy the Lion joined in
and helped pump up the
crowd.

For more information, go to
www.lmulions.com

For ticket information, go to
**100.lmu.edu/tickets**

## 2011 CENTENNIAL GAMES

**9.10.11**
Men's water polo
vs. Pepperdine

**9.29.11**
Women's volleyball vs. BYU

**10.9.11**
Women's soccer
vs. Gonzaga

**10.29.11**
Men's crew vs. UCLA

**10.29.11**
Cross-country at WCC
Championships at
Belmont, Calif.

**11.6.11**
Men's soccer vs. Gonzaga

**12.2.11**
Men's basketball
vs. Columbia

**12.4.11**
Women's basketball
vs. UCLA

**1.15.12**
Swimming vs. UC Davis

## OLD SCHOOL SPIRIT

Students will have more than a dozen chances to wave their centennial scarves and cheer the Lions as each of LMU's Division 1 teams dedicate a game in honor of the university's 100th year. LMU will face traditional foes, such as Pepperdine's baseball team and the UCLA women's basketball team, and nonconference opponents, such as the UC Davis women's swimming team and Columbia's men's basketball team. The game against Columbia, on Dec. 2, 2011, has an added dimension: It pits the Lions of the WCC against the Ivy League Lions.

Sports have played an important role in the university's life from the beginning. Baseball, football and basketball were the main sports when St. Vincent's College became Los Angeles College in 1911.

**1.21.12**
Women's basketball vs. Santa Clara

**3.10.12**
Women's rowing vs. SDSU

**3.10.12**
Women's water polo vs. UC San Diego

**3.13.12**
Softball vs. Notre Dame

**4.12.12**
Baseball vs. San Francisco

**4.14.12**
Men's tennis vs. Portland

**4.18.12**
Men's golf at WCC Championships in Hollister, Calif.

**4.20.12**
Women's tennis vs. BYU

**5.18.12**
Baseball vs. Pepperdine

■◀ Relive the birthday bash
at **100.lmu.edu/bbq**

**CENTENNIAL BBQ**

Thousands of LMU alumni descended on Sunken Garden to celebrate LMU's 100th birthday party at the 58th Annual Alumni BBQ on Sept. 25. During an afternoon of delicious food, cold beverages and fun-filled events, alumni reconnected with their friends and the faculty who inspired them, reliving old memories while creating new ones.

In the early '60s, before the merger between Loyola University and Marymount College, the Alumni BBQ was strictly a stag event. Some 200 alumni attended the BBQ, held on the former location of Sullivan Field (east of Gersten Pavilion today). They were served steak, beans and beer.

Although the BBQ has grown in many ways since then, alumni affinity for LMU has stayed the same. With special attention on the university's centennial year, this year's BBQ was yet another unforgettable celebration. From a 350-pound birthday cake to the Centennial Alumni Mass to cannons firing confetti, alumni shared in the celebration of LMU's 100 years of education in the Jesuit and Marymount traditions.

**THE COLLAGE** Visitors to the Welcome Center of the newly renovated Charles Von der Ahe Building are now greeted by a one-of-a-kind piece of art celebrating LMU's centennial. From the 1911–1912 bulletin of Los Angeles College to the Loyolan's coverage of President David W. Burcham's appointment, more than 200 artifacts and photos from the university's storied past have been reproduced in the Centennial Collage. Artist Lawrence Romorini took as his inspiration LMU's commitment to educate the whole person in the Jesuit and Marymount traditions. The three-dimensional collage presents a visual history of LMU, from its roots as St. Vincent's College, through the founding of Los Angeles College and Marymount-in-the-West School, and culminating in LMU's move into the 21st century. Flowing counterclockwise from its top, the collage weaves together symbols of the people, places and events that have shaped LMU into the institution it is today.

1 Admission ticket for an LMU men's basketball game – 1982

2 Marymount College pennant

3 Telegraph from Harry Culver to President Joseph Sullivan, S.J., confirming Culver's donation of 99 acres in the Del Rey Hills to Loyola College – 1927

4 Bulletin of Marymount School and Junior College – 1936

5 Loyola University freshman orientation beanie

6 Seal of LMU, designed by Provost Renée Harrangue, R.S.H.M., '57 in 1973

7 Bronze medallion of St. Ignatius Loyola, S.J., founder of the Society of Jesus

8 Piece of the original floor in Gersten Pavilion, used from 1981 to 2009

9 Loyola University letterman jacket – 1950

10 California Army National Guard uniform patch of Alfred Kilp, S.J., '30, chaplain during WWII with 9th Army in Europe Loyola University

11 Lapel pin of a past LMU logo – 1984

COLLAGE BY LAWRENCE ROMORINI AT ONE OF A KIND ART STUDIO

## LITURGIES CELEBRATE CENTENNIAL

The celebration of the Eucharist is at the heart of LMU's Catholic identity and mission. It is the university's primary act of worship and a symbol of its vibrant life. During the centennial year, three Eucharistic liturgies are providing LMU with opportunities to thank God for the blessings bestowed upon the university in its first 100 years and pray for the Holy Spirit's guidance. LMU commissioned a centennial hymn by Tony Alonso, M.A. '11, director of music ministry in the Peg Dolan, RSHM Campus Ministry Center, which is being sung at each of these liturgies.

CENTENNIAL MASS OF THE HOLY SPIRIT The annual celebration of the Mass of the Holy Spirit is a tradition dating back to the first European universities in the Middle Ages. Each year, Catholic universities across the globe gather to pray for the Holy Spirit's blessing as they commence the academic year. As LMU gathered for the Mass of the Holy Spirit, the university invoked the Spirit's blessing on its centennial and asked for God's guidance in the century to come.
**THURSDAY, SEPT. 22, 2011**, Noon, Sacred Heart Chapel
**PRESIDER:** Robert W. Scholla, S.J., rector of the LMU Jesuit Community
**HOMILIST:** Joseph W. LaBrie, S.J., special assistant to the president

CENTENNIAL ALUMNI MASS Each year, thousands of alumni of Loyola University, Marymount College and LMU return to campus for Alumni Reunion Weekend. After two days of reunions and gatherings, the weekend culminates in the Alumni Mass and BBQ. This year, alumni and their families came to campus to celebrate the university's first 100 years and recognize God's abundant blessings on our community.
**SUNDAY, SEPT. 25, 2011**, 10 a.m., Sacred Heart Chapel
**PRESIDER:** Richard A. Robin, S.J., special assistant to the executive director of Alumni Relations and Annual Giving
**HOMILIST:** Joseph W. LaBrie, S.J., special assistant to the president

CENTENNIAL MASS AT THE CATHEDRAL OF OUR LADY OF THE ANGELS For 100 years, LMU has cherished its role in the archdiocese as the city's Catholic university. LMU invites the greater Los Angeles community to join the university in celebrating our centennial at the Cathedral of Our Lady of the Angels during a special Eucharistic liturgy. Archbishop José Gomez will serve as the principal celebrant and homilist, and Cardinal Roger Mahony, archbishop emeritus, will serve as the presider.
**SATURDAY, APRIL 14, 2012**, 3 p.m., Cathedral of Our Lady of the Angels
**PRINCIPAL CELEBRANT AND HOMILIST:** The Most Rev. José H. Gomez, archbishop of Los Angeles
**PRESIDER:** His Eminence, Cardinal Roger M. Mahony, archbishop emeritus of Los Angeles

**CENTENNIAL HYMN**
Through every generation
you nourish and sustain
your people,blessed and
  broken,
through every joy and pain.

You weave our many stories
as one, though many parts.
You shape us as one body
within your sacred heart:

That all may have life,
that all may be one,
that all we believe
and all we become
may be for the glory,
the greater glory,
may be for the glory of God.

**—TONY ALONSO, MA '11**
excerpt from a hymn
commissioned for LMU's
centennial year

## 11.11.11 BALL

LMU is throwing a Centennial Ball for the student body, harkening back to the early days of Loyola College. Inspired by an archival photo of students and young alumni sporting tuxes and ball gowns, the formal dinner dance will be held on Nov. 11, 2011, (11.11.11) at the Millenium Biltmore Hotel in downtown Los Angeles. Already lending its historical charm, the Biltmore ballroom will be decorated with archival LMU photos, connecting students to those years past. A short toast at 11:11 p.m. will cap the festivities.

*Loyola College. Alumni Ball. Fiesta Room, The Ambassador. April 25-1924.*

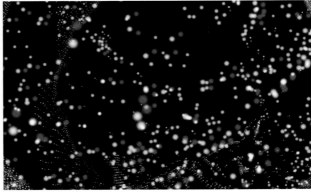

THE OPUS PRIZE CELEBRATES COMMITMENT TO SOCIAL JUSTICE LMU is proud to partner with the Opus Prize Foundation in recognizing three faith-based social entrepreneurs who address some of the world's greatest social problems. The Opus Prize grants one $1 million prize and two $100,000 finalist awards. The university solicited nominations from around the world, and assembled a jury of community leaders chaired by President David W. Burcham. The Opus Prize winner will be announced at the ceremony.

**OPUS PRIZE AWARDS CEREMONY**
Nov. 2, 2011
Burns Backcourt, Fritz B. Burns Recreation Center
7 p.m.
**www.lmu.edu/opus**

LMU FACULTY ENSHRINED IN A HALL OF FAME LMU is commemorating the centennial by dedicating a Faculty Hall of Fame. The hall calls attention to meaningful contributions of teaching, scholarship and service by our faculty. Any eligible LMU faculty member, including those who taught at Marymount College and Loyola University, may be nominated.

**FACULTY HALL OF FAME**
Learn more at
100.lmu.edu/fame

HAIL! THE CRIMSON AND THE BLUE! LMU sang its new Alma Mater during the 2011 commencement. The lyrics are written by English professor Kelly Younger '94 and Rachel Van Houten '03. Daniel Dangca '11, who led the Alma Mater's premiere, said, "It's a refreshing reminder of our vibrant tradition, but also a call for a mindful new beginning."

**HAIL! THE CRIMSON AND THE BLUE!**
Memorize the lyrics at
100.lmu.edu/almamater

THREE WINES COMMEMORATE 100 YEARS LMU proudly introduced three commemorative wines: Mendocino chardonnay, "Old Vines" zinfandel and a 2006 Mount Veeder cabernet sauvignon. The Mendocino chardonnay is produced by Steve Brutocao '86 at his Brutocao Cellars. Alum Chris Silva produces the "Old Vines" zinfandel with grapes from vines planted more than 100 years ago. The Mt. Veeder Cabernet Sauvignon is produced by Robert Craig of Robert Craig Winery, a long-time participant in the LMU Wine Classic. The centennial wine labels were designed by LMU studio arts students Jessica Wong and Kaitlin De la Cruz.

**CENTENNIAL WINE**
Order yours at
100.lmu.edu/wine

STUDENTS, FACULTY, ALUMNI ARE INSPIRED BY CENTENNIAL The Laband Art Gallery's ART 100 showcase celebrates the centennial year with three exhibits. The alumni exhibition in the fall includes works from College of Communication and Fine Arts graduates over the past four decades. In the spring, the studio arts faculty demonstrates the range of talent and technique taught in the department. The third exhibition features work by current students encompassing various types of media.

**ART 100**
View exhibit details at
cfa.lmu.edu/laband

CENTENNIAL DAY OF SERVICE PUTS LMU TO WORK LMU's mission statement boldly declares a commitment to the service of faith and promotion of justice. Our mission is lived each day as students and alumni work with those in their communities who are most in need. As part of the centennial year celebration, LMU honors this commitment and the goal to form women and men for others with a Centennial Day of Service.

**CENTENNIAL DAY OF SERVICE**
March 24, 2012
Get more information at
100.lmu.edu/serviceday

Loyola University Site
May 20th 1928

The undeveloped Del Rey Hills in 1928 are the future home of the Westchester campus.

# LMU:
## A Centennial History

*From the inevitable to the improbable, excerpts from our dramatic first century.*

**BY KEVIN STARR**

*From the front lines of war to the edge of financial collapse to student unrest, LMU has risen to the challenges of time, evolving with a changing world while staying true to its values. The following excerpts from the definitive "Loyola Marymount University, 1911–2011: A Centennial History," by award-winning author and California historian Kevin Starr, provide a glimpse into our dramatic first century. Visit 100.lmu.edu to order and enjoy the complete chronicle.*

IN THE BEGINNING THERE WAS A MAN WITH A PLAN. All things considered, Bishop Conaty did not have a problem with St. Vincent's as a viable, serviceable high school and college. Still, he wanted more. He wanted an ambitious Catholic university. (*Learn about Conaty's vision for the Jesuits in the Southland in Chapter 1.*)

ONE COLLEGE, TWO NAME CHANGES AND TWO LOCATIONS LATER. Thus commenced academic year 1917-1918 for the Jesuit institution still called St. Vincent's College. At the dedicatory ceremony, in fact, Father Ruppert explicitly stated that the name St. Vincent's would always be cherished. He spoke too soon. Certain members of the Jesuit community favored a new start in name as well as building. Such a preference was neither superficial nor without consequences. The first name under which the Jesuits began secondary instruction, Los Angeles College, linked the institution to the city. The name change to St. Vincent's College in 1914 allowed the Jesuits to acquire the ability under the state charter of the old St. Vincent's College to grant bachelor's, master's and doctoral degrees, as well as to enjoy the tax-exempt status of the Vincentian institution. But neither name projected an assertive Jesuit identity, hence the gathering of sentiment behind the name Loyola College on the part of the Jesuit community as 1918 approached. (*But changing the name meant breaking a promise. Read how in Chapter 3.*)

WHILE THE TWENTIES ROARED, THE COLLEGE GREW. IT LITERALLY COULDN'T CONTAIN ITSELF. BUT HOW AND WHERE TO EXPAND? A cavalcade of run-on sentences and sentence fragments, [developer] Harry Culver's telegram of 19 October 1927 to Father Sullivan,

**LOYOLA MARYMOUNT UNIVERSITY, 1911–2011: A Centennial History**

By Kevin Starr
Wilsted and Taylor publisher
9 x 12, hardback
560 pages
$100
Available at the LMU Bookstore and online at
100.lmu.edu/book

**FRONT LINE LIONS**
A plaque commemorating Lions who made the ultimate sacrifice in World War II was affixed to the Memorial Gymnasium in 1948.

**LORENZO MALONE, S.J.,** Loyola football supporter and World War II civilian adjunct chaplain, was Dean of Students.

sent at 7:08 p.m., was at best quasi-coherent. It did, however, make a momentous offer, one hundred acres on the western edge of the city, free of charge, for a new Loyola campus.

Nor was the Playa Del Rey district the best locality in the city, as Sullivan described it to his provincial. It was, in point of fact, an ultra-remote region, devoid of any streetcar connection to the population centers of the city—devoid, in fact, of paved roads, sewers, sidewalks, streetlights, and electricity. A Big Red Car ran north and south between Santa Monica and Redondo Beach, but neither of these communities was a large population center. Loyola College was a commuter school. How were students to reach a campus perched atop a remote mesa? (*How indeed. And how would they pay for it? Find out in Chapter 4.*)

DESPITE THE COLLEGE'S FINANCIAL WOES, THE CITY WAS GROWING, THE OCEAN WAS SHINING, THE FUTURE WAS BRIGHT. AT LEAST UNTIL TUESDAY. And then, on the morning of 29 October 1929, Black Tuesday, the stock market—following a week of crisis, which in turn was building upon a nearly year-long downturn in the business cycle—having plummeted on the twenty-fourth and then showed signs of recovery, crashed catastrophically. The bottom fell out of the market. Stocks spiraled down to oblivion. An era of speculation—the kind of speculation upon which the Del Rey venture was based—had come to an end, and the ensuing Depression would bring Loyola University to the brink of extinction, or at the least to an abandonment of the Del Rey campus and a forced regrouping of itself on Venice Boulevard. (*How does football figure into a deep depression? Surprisingly well. See for yourself in Chapters 5-7.*)

WHAT COULD POSSIBLY BE WORSE THAN THE LOSS OF FINANCIAL SUPPORT IN THE MIDDLE OF A DEPRESSION? YOUNG LOYOLANS WERE ABOUT TO FIND OUT. News came in and was duly reported of Loyolans running into each other in faraway places, on front lines, in rest areas, or on leave; of Loyolans recovering from wounds in field hospitals or long-term care facilities on the home front; and, sadly, of Loyolans making the supreme sacrifice in battle or dying in accidents. In these letters—news-filled, nostalgic, heartfelt, sometimes frightened, nearly always animated by hope for the postwar future—Loyolans reminisced about their time in the Del Rey Hills, asked after this or that teacher, described what they were doing (within the parameters established by military censorship), expressed gratitude for past favors, struggled with the question of what they would do with their future (provided they had one), talked about impromptu reunions with other Loyolans encountered in transit or at duty stations, and again and again expressed their gratitude to [Father] Malone for their time at Loyola and the memories of Loyola that now sustained them and, always, asked his prayers for their safety. (*For in-depth coverage of the Front Line Lions program, see Chapter 9.*)

A generation at war across the globe would in time be designated the Greatest Generation. Front Line Lions played their part, and on the home front the university remembered them and kept in touch.

Circa 1970, Loyola University and Marymount College were two affiliated institutions on the same campus.

TWO DECADES LATER, A DIFFERENT BATTLE WOULD ENSUE AND A DOOR WOULD BE OPENED. BUT WHO WOULD WALK THROUGH IT AND HOW FAR WOULD THEY BE ALLOWED TO GO? Large Jesuit universities in urban settings especially favored coeducation, yet smaller and more remote colleges were making plans as well. The trouble was, Cardinal McIntyre—as he informed Father Casassa in at least one earlier interview—did not approve of Loyola going coeducational; indeed, the cardinal did not approve of coeducation, period. Coeducation was against the traditions of Catholic education, the cardinal believed, aside from the fact that a coeducational Loyola would prove a competitive threat to the Catholic women's colleges of the archdiocese. (*Game was on, one might say. Read how it plays out in Chapter 23.*)

As of early November, however, the name "Loyola University and Marymount College" was still being used by Loyola, while Sister McKay and the Marymount community were calling the institution "Loyola/Marymount University." Father Merrifield opposed this amalgamated name in a letter to chairman Sanchez, whom Merrifield feared was softening on the matter of nomenclature. "I feel, as I am sure the majority of faculty do," Merrifield wrote Sanchez on 27 November 1972, "that the Marymount name neither belongs on nor will be anything but a handicap for the Colleges of Science and Engineering, the College of Business Administration, the Graduate Division, and the Law School. I realize it is not easy to come to a solution—but 'peace at any price' seems to be part of your present mood."

Merrifield resisted the Loyola/Marymount University name throughout the holiday season. "I do think we are giving away the store," he wrote Father Terrance Mahan on 11 December 1972, "and getting little in return." (*See what "giving away the store" can get you in Chapter 25.*)

DURING A TUMULTUOUS 1965-1975, NATIONAL UNREST DESCENDED UPON LOYOLA PROMPTING STUDENTS TO SPEAK UP, MARCH AND EVEN TAKE OVER THE DEVELOPMENT OFFICE. Finally, on 13 May 1970, a group of fifteen students broke off from an impressive peace march of some 750 marchers and seized the university development office.

During the afternoon and evening of that Tuesday, the number occupying the building swelled to more than 200. The protest was originally against the expansion of the war in Vietnam but soon turned into a demand for increased minority scholarships and other related affirmative action programs.

Throughout the proceedings, the new university president played a risky game. He knew, for one thing, that he could not let a group of 50 to 100 protesters occupy an office filled with files containing privileged information about Loyola benefactors as well as other confidential matters. Many conservative faculty, lay and Jesuit alike, wanted Merrifield to order the police in to clear the space by 5:00 p.m., just about the time that Merrifield was ordering out for hamburgers. (*He fed them? Find out what happened next in Chapter 26.*)

**TOGETHER AT LAST**
The sign at the entrance to campus in 1968 said it all: two independent but affiliated institutions were operating at the same location.

Recruitment publication, circa 1974.

The state-of-the-art, $63-million William H. Hannon Library opened in September 2009.

HAVING REORGANIZED AND REFINED ITS ACADEMICS, A RENEWED UNIVERSITY SEEKS TO BUILD ITS FUTURE. BUT NOT WITHOUT SOME NEIGHBORLY OPPOSITION. On 17 June 1983 Hughes Aircraft, a Delaware corporation, and Loyola Marymount University, a California nonprofit corporation, signed an agreement transferring from Hughes to LMU a twenty-eight-and-a half-acre parcel of land contiguous to the western boundary of the campus. (*Does this "Louisiana Purchase" lead to a flourishing university or just traffic congestion? See Chapter 29 for details.*)

Of all the groups LMU had faced, LMU Neighbors was the best organized and most recalcitrant. Far from being primarily interested in parking and road access—matters that had been by and large settled—LMU Neighbors was opposed to the notion of developing the Leavey campus, especially the bluffs, with residence halls. Even more confrontationally, the group accused LMU of not significantly adjusting its development program throughout eight years of give and take with neighborhood groups. Father Loughran, now in the final months of his presidency, debated the charges in a number of privately circulated letters and memos. (*How does LMU overcome resistance? According to Chapter 30, very carefully.*)

AS THE MILLENNIUM TURNS, THE UNIVERSITY MUST EVOLVE OR BE LEFT BEHIND. WHAT CHANGES NEED TO BE MADE AND WHAT WILL STAND THE TEST OF TIME? By the turn of the millennium, though Jesuits were fewer than in times past, LMU coupled its Marymount tradition—an emphasis on the arts, the effective presence of R.S.H.M. and C.S.J. religious in teaching and campus ministry, and, most of all, the vital and vitalizing presence of women undergraduates—with Jesuit service and values. (*Distinguished Jesuit academics endure. Chapter 32 explains how.*)

As tentative plans continued through the final years of O'Malley's administration and the first years of Lawton's, it became apparent that the Charles Von Der Ahe Library and its atrium annex could not be further enlarged, lest the structure become a multi-level hodgepodge prohibitive of smooth operation. An entirely new library was needed.

At current costs, this construction meant something in the range of $63 million. In the last years of his administration, O'Malley and his staff lined up a potential donor for nearly a third of the projected cost, but that prospect fell through. A new library now became Lawton's responsibility; indeed, it became the defining project of his administration. (*But $60 million doesn't grow on trees. Chapter 34 has the story.*)

More than eighty years after Harry Culver first made his gift, the LMU campus now encompassed 142 acres. Time and history had domesticated an empty mesa. Raw acreage had been transformed into a landscaped garden. Two isolated buildings had evolved into a harmonious architectural composition. Yet the work was not complete; it would never be completed. LMU would never become fixed in time. (*What's next for LMU? Find out in Chapter 34.*)

Read more LMU history in the interactive timeline at **100.lmu.edu/timeline**

# The Road to 100

**1865**

**ST. VINCENT'S COLLEGE** Bishop Thaddeus Amat y Brusi, C.M., invites the Company of the Missions (Vincentian Fathers) to open the first institution of higher education in Los Angeles. That year, they open St. Vincent's College at the Lugo family's former townhouse on the Los Angeles Plaza, at the end of Olvera Street. John Asmuth, C.M., is the first president. Over the next 46 years, the school occupies four locations in the downtown Los Angeles neighborhood, including the site now known as St. Vincent's Plaza.

**1915**

**BACK TO ST. VINCENT'S COLLEGE** Los Angeles College changes its name back to St. Vincent's College.

**1915**

**FREDERICK RUPPERT, S.J.,** is named the third president of the College.

**1916**

**GROUNDBREAKING** Rather than breaking ground on a new campus in Hollywood, as had been expected, the college breaks ground on Venice Boulevard in the Pico Heights District.

**1917**

**PICO HEIGHTS** The college moves to its new campus in the Pico Heights District; today, it is the campus of Loyola High School.

**1923**

**1923**

**THE LIONS** Loyola College formally adopts the lion as its mascot.

**MARYMOUNT-IN-THE-WEST** At Bishop John Cantwell's invitation, Cecilia Rafter, R.S.H.M., and six sisters of the Religious of the Sacred Heart of Mary move to Los Angeles and welcome seven students to Marymount-in-the-West. Its first location is the Brockman Estate in downtown Los Angeles, now home to a USC sorority.

**1926**

**1928**

**THE DEL REY GROUNDBREAKING** Religious, civic, business and academic leaders from throughout the state participate in the groundbreaking of Loyola's new campus in the Del Rey Hills.

**1929**

**LOYOLA UNIVERSITY** Loyola College incorporates as Loyola University at its new campus in Del Rey. St. Robert Bellarmine Hall and St. Francis Xavier Hall, housing both students and Jesuits, are the first two structures on the new campus. The high school division remains at the Pico Heights campus and the law school moves to the Byrne Building in downtown Los Angeles.

**1929**

**CRIMSON CIRCLE** The first service organization, Crimson Circle, is formed by Loyola's dean of students, Lorenzo M. Malone, S.J., '17.

**1930**

**ZACHEUS J. MAHER, S.J.,** is named the sixth president of Loyola University.

**1911**

**THE FOUNDING: LOS ANGELES COLLEGE**
Bishop Thomas Conaty invites the Society of Jesus to take over St. Vincent's College. Not wishing to assume the massive debt of the college, they close the school and open Los Angeles College in the Highland Park neighborhood, transferring most of the students from St. Vincent's. Richard Gleeson, S.J., is named the first president. St. Vincent's College alumnus Isidore Dockweiler 1887 is appointed as the first lay member of Los Angeles College Board of Trustees.

**1914**

**WILLIAM J. DEENEY, S.J.**, is named the second president of Los Angeles College.

**1918**

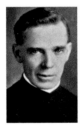

**HENRY WELCH, S.J.**, is named the fourth president of the college.

**1918**

**LOYOLA COLLEGE** The name changes to Loyola College.

**1920**

**THE LAW SCHOOL** is founded as St. Vincent's School of Law, welcoming both women and men. It is the first law school in Los Angeles to admit students of all faiths.

**1920**

**LOS ANGELES LOYOLAN** The Cinder in the Public's Eye begins publication as the first student newspaper. It would soon change its name to the Los Angeles Loyolan.

**1926**

**JOSEPH A. SULLIVAN, S.J.**, is named the fifth president of Loyola College.

**THE CULVER GIFT** Harry Culver donates 100 acres of land in the Del Rey Hills (now Westchester) to Loyola College for a new campus.

**1927**

**ACADEMIC EXPANSION** Loyola's original academic college, the College of Arts and Sciences (now the Bellarmine College of Liberal Arts) is joined by the School of Commerce and Finance (now the College of Business Administration) and School of Engineering (later developed into the Frank R. Seaver College of Science and Engineering). The new schools provide the foundation for the college's traditional immigrant classes (Basques, Italians, Irish, Filipinos and Sonoran Mexicans) to enter into the professional world of Los Angeles.

**1930**

**COACH THOMAS LIEB** Knute Rockne, recruited by Loyola to create the "Notre Dame of the West," comes to campus for the shooting of his biopic on location at Loyola's Sullivan Field. Rockne declined the coaching job, but his protégé and assistant, Thomas Lieb, was instead named athletic director and head coach of the football and ice hockey teams.

# LMU100 The Road to 100

## 1931

**WESTWOOD**
Marymount-in-the-West relocates to a 7 acre campus on the north side of UCLA in Westwood.

## 1931

## 1932

**THE DEL REY PLAYERS**, a student theatre troupe, forms at Loyola.

## 1937

## 1938

**CHARLES A. MCQUILLAN, S.J.**, is named the eighth president of Loyola University.

## 1945

**A GRAVE INJUSTICE** Recognizing the injustice of the internment of Japanese Americans during WWII, President Whelan hires many individuals returning from the camps who had lost their homes and jobs. Apartments are built for their families in the basement of St. Robert's Hall.

## 1945

**THE G.I. BILL** The Loyola University campus population begins to explode due to the GI Bill. The current campus infrastructure is unable to accommodate everyone so temporary Quonset huts are constructed in Sunken Garden.

## 1946

**FRANK SULLIVAN** is named professor of English at Loyola University, beginning his storied career at the university spanning more than 30 years.

## 1948

## 1949

**CHARLES S. CASASSA, S.J.**, is named the 10th president of Loyola University.

## 1950

**LION FOOTBALL** Don Klosterman '51 breaks two national college football records, completing 26 of 51 passes in a game. The football team, ranked 19th in the nation and poised to receive an invitation to play in the Orange Bowl, forfeits a game in protest at Texas Western College because Loyola's African-American team members were not allowed on the field.

## 1952

**ALPHA DELTA GAMMA** opens as the first national fraternity chapter at Loyola.

**1932**

**GRAND AVENUE**
The law school moves from the Byrne Building to a new home on South Grand Avenue.

**HUGH C. DUCE, S.J.**, is named the seventh president of Loyola University.

**1933**

**MARYMOUNT JUNIOR COLLEGE** opens on the Westwood campus. Gertrude Cain, R.S.H.M., is the first president.

**1935**

**THE LOYOLA BAND** John Boudreau starts the Loyola Band.

---

**1942**

**LION HOCKEY**
The Lions defeat USC to win their third consecutive Pacific Coast League Ice Hockey Championship.

**EDWARD J. WHELAN, S.J.**, is named the ninth president of Loyola University.

**1948**

**MARYMOUNT COLLEGE** is chartered as a four-year college.

**ALUMNI MEMORIAL GYM** opens as one of the largest basketball arenas in the West.

**1942–45**

**WORLD WAR II** To save the university from closing during World War II, President Whelan incorporates the Government Wartime Program to train military officers during an accelerated academic program. This program would soon become Army Air Corps ROTC, now AFROTC.

---

**1953**

**SACRED HEART CHAPEL** is built. The tower is added a year later due to radar-blocking concerns that might affect the Hughes runway below the bluff.

**1953**

**ST. JOSEPH TEACHER COLLEGE OF ORANGE** is established by the Sisters of St. Joseph of Orange as an affiliate junior college of the Catholic University of America. It is originally a teacher preparation school exclusively for women religious.

**WORKSHOP IN HUMAN RELATIONS,** later named the Martin Gang Institute, opens. It promoted the interdisciplinary and comprehensive understanding of racial cooperation in Southern California. Then–LAPD officer Tom Bradley, mayor of Los Angeles from 1973 to 1993, is among the workshop's first graduates. Bradley would remain lifelong friends with President Charles Casassa, S.J., and later say that the workshop changed his life and his view of race relations in Los Angeles.

**AQUINAS BROWN, R.S.H.M.,** is named the second president of Marymount College.

**ST. JOSEPH COLLEGE OF ORANGE** is established as a four-year institution with Mary Felix Montgomery, C.S.J., as the president.

**THE CHARLES VON DER AHE LIBRARY** opens.

**THE FRANK R. SEAVER HALL OF SCIENCE** opens to house biology, chemistry and physics.

**THE SECOND VATICAN COUNCIL** takes place in Rome. Future Professor of Theological Studies Herbert J. Ryan, S.J., serves as secretary to theologian John Courtney Murray, S.J., and peritus to Cardinal Francis Spellman, archbishop of New York, during the second, third and fourth sessions of the council.

**FOLEY HALL** Edward T. Foley Hall opens, including the Charles H. Strub Memorial Theatre.

**PROFESSOR GEORGE DUNNE, S.J.** Pope Paul VI and the Rev. Eugene Carson Blake, general secretary of the World Council of Churches, name George Dunne, S.J., '26, professor of political science at Loyola, as the first Secretary-General of the Committee on Society, Development and Peace in Geneva. It is the first joint enterprise by the Roman Catholic and Protestant churches since the Reformation.

**THE GRYPHON CIRCLE** is formed at Marymount College as its first service organization.

**THE MARYMOUNT COLLEGE AGREEMENT** Presidents Raymunde McKay, R.S.H.M., and Mary Felix Montgomery, C.S.J., sign the Marymount College Agreement. The agreement merges Marymount College and St. Joseph College of Orange under the Marymount name with both the R.S.H.M. and St. Joseph sisters co-equally administering the school under President McKay's leadership.

| 1955 | 1957 | | 1957 | 1958 |

**PEREIRA HALL** The John Pereira, S.J., Hall of Engineering opens, honoring the Jesuit brother who planted all of the original trees on campus.

**GERTRUDE CAIN, R.S.H.M.**, returns to Marymount College as its third president.

KXLU 88.9 F.M. RADIO began broadcasting

**THE STUDENT WORKERS PROGRAM** is established by Thomas O'Rourke, S.J., to assist students with financial need.

**THE MALONE CENTER** The Lorenzo M. Malone, S.J., Student Center opens.

| 1960 | 1960 | 1960 | |

**MARIE DU SACRE COUER SMITH, R.S.H.M.**, is named the fourth president of Marymount College.

**PALOS VERDES** Marymount College moves to a new campus in Palos Verdes.

**THE BELLES** form as a women's service organization. The group originally is comprised of students from five Catholic women's colleges including Marymount College.

| 1964 | 1966 | |

**PRESIDENT RAYMUNDE MCKAY, R.S.H.M.**, is named the fifth president of Marymount College.

**WEST NINTH STREET** Loyola Law School moves from South Grand Avenue to a new campus on West Ninth Street.

**NEGOTIATIONS BEGIN** Presidents Charles Casassa, S.J., of Loyola University, and Raymunde McKay, R.S.H.M., of Marymount College, begin discussions with Cardinal James McIntyre, archbishop of Los Angeles, about the prospect of an affiliation between the two schools.

| 1968 | 1968 |

**THE LOYOLA–MARYMOUNT AFFILIATION** Presidents Charles Casassa, S.J., of Loyola University, and Raymunde McKay, R.S.H.M., of Marymount College, announce that Marymount will move its four-year programs from Palos Verdes and Orange to Loyola's Westchester campus as Loyola and Marymount begin their affiliation. Marymount's two-year programs remain at their other campuses.

**BSU AND UMAS** The Black Student Union and United Mexican-American Students form.

**1969**

**PRESIDENT DONALD P. MERRIFIELD, S.J.,** is named the 11th president of Loyola University.

**1969**

**THE LEAVEY CENTER** is dedicated as the official residence of the Religious of the Sacred Heart of Mary. The Sisters of St. Joseph of Orange originally share the facility but would soon move to their own communities in the Westchester neighborhood.

**1970**

**1973**

**LOYOLA MARYMOUNT UNIVERSITY** Loyola University and Marymount College formally merge into Loyola Marymount University. Donald P. Merrifield, S.J., continues to serve as president and Marymount Academic Vice President Renée Harrangue, R.S.H.M., '57 is named provost.

**1973**

**THE COLLEGE OF COMMUNICATION AND FINE ARTS** forms at LMU, comprised primarily of departments brought to Westchester by Marymount College.

**1974**

**HILLEL**, a national Jewish student organization, forms on campus.

**1974**

**NA KOLEA** forms on campus and begins hosting its annual luau for the LMU and Westchester communities.

**1980**

**THE GEHRY REDESIGN** The Frank Gehry-designed remodel of Loyola Law School begins.

**1980**

**MARITAL AND FAMILY THERAPY** When Immaculate Heart College closes, its Department of Clinical Art Therapy (now the Graduate Department of Marital and Family Therapy) moves to LMU.

**1982**

**THE CENTER FOR SERVICE AND ACTION** The Educational Participation in Communities Program, renamed the Center for Service and Action in 2000, is established.

**1983**

**THE LEAVEY CAMPUS**, adjacent to the original 100 acres of land donated by Harry Culver, is purchased. It later becomes the site of six student residence halls and the William H. Hannon Library.

**1984**

**XXIII OLYMPIC GAMES** Gersten Pavilion hosts the weightlifting competition for the XXIII Olympic Summer Games.

**THE STUDENT GOVERNMENTS MERGE,** forming a joint governing body, the Associated Students of Loyola and Marymount, and elect a Marymount student as president.

**COMMUNICATION ARTS** The Wil and Mary Jane Von Der Ahe Communication Arts Building opens.

**THE BIRD NEST** opens on the university bluff as a venue for student events. It is named in honor of Richard Robin, S.J., former dean of men, director of housing and longtime assistant to the president.

**ALPHA PHI** A chapter of Alpha Phi opens as the first sorority at LMU.

**APSA** The Asian Pacific Student Association forms.

**SPECIAL GAMES** The first Special Games, now the largest annual service project, is held at LMU.

**VON DER AHE EXPANSION** The Charles Von der Ahe Library completes major expansion, doubling its size.

**JAMES FOXWORTHY,** professor of engineering, is named executive vice president.

**PROFESSOR HERBERT J. RYAN, S.J.** In recognition of his work toward Anglican–Catholic unity as a member of the historic First Anglican–Roman Catholic International Commission, Herbert J. Ryan, S.J., professor of theological studies, is awarded the Cross of the Order of St. Augustine of Canterbury by Archbishop Robert Runcie of Canterbury a year after receiving the Pontifical Medal of Merit by Pope John Paul II. He previously received the International Christian Unity Award in 1974.

**JOAN TREACY, R.S.H.M., '67** is named Provost.

**JAMES LOUGHRAN, S.J.,** is named the 12th president of LMU.

**THE BURNS FINE ARTS CENTER** opens.

**THE RAINS GIFT** Lilliore Green Rains leaves the university $45 million in her will, the largest gift in the history of the university.

| 1986 | 1988 | 1990 |
|---|---|---|

**PROVOST MARY MILLIGAN, R.S.H.M.** The former General Superior of the Religious of the Sacred Heart of Mary, Mary Milligan, R.S.H.M., is named provost.

**THE BURNS CAMPUS** The upper campus is named after long-time friend and benefactor Fritz B. Burns.

**LION BASKETBALL** The men's basketball team, led by seniors Bo Kimble and Jeff Fryer, reaches the Elite Eight of the NCAA Tournament, after the death of star player Hank Gathers during the WCC Tournament at Gersten Pavilion.

| 1995 | 1998 |
|---|---|

**THE HILTON CENTER** opens as the new home of the College of Business Administration.

**ALUMNI FOR OTHERS,** a nationwide service program for alumni, is founded by Peg Dolan, R.S.H.M., '58, M.A. '74.

| 1999 | 2000 |
|---|---|

**SCHOOL OF FILM AND TELEVISION** is chartered from the College of Communication and Fine Arts.

**SCHOOL OF EDUCATION** is chartered.

| 2008 | 2008 | 2008 |
|---|---|---|

**DAVID W. BURCHAM, LAW '84,** dean of Loyola Law School, is named executive vice president and provost.

**PEG DOLAN, R.S.H.M., CAMPUS MINISTRY CENTER AND PROGRAM** are named in honor of Peg Dolan, R.S.H.M., '58, M.A. '74, former director of campus ministry and alumni chaplain.

**PEACE JAM** Six Nobel Peace Prize Laureates, including Archbishop Desmond Tutu of South Africa, address a packed Gersten Pavilion as part of the Peace Jam Conference.

**1990**

**THE MUSLIM STUDENT ASSOCIATION** forms at LMU.

**1991**

**THOMAS P. O'MALLEY, S.J.,** is named the 13th president of LMU.

**1992**

**LEAVEY GROUNDBREAKING** LMU breaks ground on construction for the Leavey Campus. During construction a year later, a significant archaeological discovery of American Indian artifacts is revealed.

**1999**

**JESUITS AND R.S.H.M. MOVE** After 70 years in Xavier Hall, the LMU Jesuit Community moves into the new Jesuit Community Complex. The Religious of the Sacred Heart of Mary move their provincial center to Montebello, and the sisters move into several smaller communities in the Westchester neighborhood after 30 years in the Leavey Center.

**1999**

**ROBERT B. LAWTON, S.J.,** is named the 14th president of LMU.

**1999**

**UNIVERSITY HALL** is purchased and opens the following year.

**TONGVA MEMORIAL** is dedicated on the bluff of the Leavey Campus in honor of the first inhabitants of the Del Rey Hills.

**2001**

**2003**

**THE ED.D.** The first doctoral program, the School of Education's Ed.D. in Educational Leadership for Social Justice, is established with an initial cohort admitted in 2004.

**2007**

**ELIE WIESEL** Nobel Peace Prize Laureate and Holocaust survivor Elie Wiesel addresses a capacity crowd at Gersten Pavilion.

**2009**

**THE WILLIAM H. HANNON LIBRARY** opens. A year later the plaza adjacent to the library is dedicated as the Robert B. Lawton, S.J. Plaza in honor of the president who oversaw the building of the library.

**2010**

**DAVID W. BURCHAM, LAW '84,** is named the 15th president of LMU.

# ORAL HISTORY PROJECT

*53 stories and counting.*
*What's yours?*

*They put in an antiaircraft battery right out by the football field. And they had a squadron of P-38s out at the airport and they were flying over the school all the time.* —Henry Bodkin Jr., 1943

*I'm thinking of five friends right now: I think of Catholics, a Protestant, an atheist and a Jew. At no point did anyone feel they were being forced to accept the idea of the other. But at the same time, we were given an environment in which we could have the discussions, which included questions about God.* —Sean Tierney, 2009

Raised in different worlds during different times, Henry and Sean's experiences couldn't be further apart. Yet what may be most compelling is what they have in common: life-shaping experiences at LMU — experiences captured in the pages of LMU's Oral History Project.

In 2010, seven LMU students set out to chronicle the stories of current and past LMU alumni, faculty and administrators. The resulting Oral History Project is a collection of learning, leading and serving — stories reflecting our commitment to academic excellence, education of the whole person, and the service of faith and promotion of justice.

The project's stories, spanning seven decades, are insightful, illuminating and inspiring. From the achievements of athletes both on and off the field, to the Loyola-Marymount merger, to a campus experiencing both physical and spiritual growth, they reveal a university that has come a very long way. They also reflect the changing world at large — a world in the throes of war, civil unrest, ethical challenges and racial discord.

The Oral History Project is chock-full of downloadable centennial articles, insights from student interviewers and complete interview transcripts, including those of Henry and Sean. Read them all at 100.lmu.edu/history.

Be a part of LMU history by contributing your special LMU memory on the Share Your Story web page at 100.lmu.edu/share. Contributions will be added to the university archives.

**GOING DOWN IN HISTORY**
Over the course of a year and a half Professor Laurie Pintar guided seven LMU history students through the process of completing the Oral History Project. During that time, Kayla Begg '12, Payton Lyon '12, Brendan McNerney '12, Michael Petersen '12, Ariana Quinonez '12, Linying Sakamoto '11 and Justin Velez '11 interviewed more than 50 members of the LMU community.

# 1940s

HENRY BODKIN JR. '43 ON LOYOLA DURING WWII [In January 1942,] we discovered that the Navy had a program designated V-7, which would allow college students, if they signed up, to finish college, then go to reserve midshipman school and be commissioned an ensign. So a whole bunch of us went down and enlisted. … We were supposed to graduate in June of '43, but we discovered that we were going to have to go to summer school and graduate early, [in February.] … Within a couple of weeks 17 of us got orders to go to midshipman school [at Columbia]. On about the 18th of February, we all got on the train at Union Station and went to New York. We arrived there, as I recall, on Washington's Birthday in a snowstorm.

# 1950s

EDISON MIYAWAKI '52 ON BEING THE FIRST ASIAN-AMERICAN AT LOYOLA To be very honest, it was a difficult time. My youthful days were in Japan, so my major language was Japanese. ... I was there primarily for an education, so I did not really get into the war situation. ... I was the first Asian on campus, so it was difficult. It was difficult to get adjusted. And I was lonesome. I didn't know anyone. But there were some very, very good families there, good dormitory mates.

AGNES MARIE SCHON, C.S.J., '54 ON BEING ONE OF THE FIRST WOMEN RELIGIOUS AT LOYOLA I was very happy to go to Loyola. And the time that I went, it was the first summer they had ever opened it to women. I think most of the women on campus for that occasion were women religious. And so I was in the first group to start. [I was] very excited to go there because it was a Jesuit university, and none of the sisters had gone to Loyola.

# 1960s

GAIL LAMMERSON BELT '60 ON BEING A STUDENT AT MARYMOUNT'S WESTWOOD CAMPUS On a typical day, you would be up by 8 or 9 a.m. and if ... you came back from your first class at 10, or any time, and you hadn't made the bed before you left, your room was locked. You had to go find the dean of students to get into your room. ... We were like all kids; we tried to get all our classes in the morning, so we could head for the beach in the afternoon.

R. CHAD DREIER '69 ON BEING AT LOYOLA DURING VIETNAM When I started in '65, ROTC was mandatory for everybody. It didn't make any difference if you were a freshman or a sophomore, you were in ROTC. They had the draft lottery in those days, and I had high draft numbers. I knew I was going in the service [so I] stayed in ROTC. The difference between Iraq and Vietnam, as a student, is that then you didn't have a choice; you were drafted.

# 1970s

LANE BOVE '69, M. ED. '72 ON BEING A MARY-MOUNT STUDENT DURING THE AFFILIATION The duties were the same as the student body president today. My office [as Marymount College student body president] was on the fourth floor of [Malone]. And most of the time was spent collaborating with the Loyola University student government — or fighting them. When the women came on campus, the men outnumbered us. There was that sense that we had to maintain our distinctiveness and be strong, so that we wouldn't be subsumed by them.

HON. IRMA BROWN DILLON '70, LAW '73 ON BEING AFRICAN-AMERICAN AT MARYMOUNT I think there were five identifiable African-American females in my class of 85. And I think of the five, maybe only three of us were openly identified and chose to be identified. It was a culture shock in many aspects. There was a level and degree of wealth that none of us had ever known. We were with upper-middle class and very wealthy young ladies who had come from very different backgrounds than ours.

# 1970s

MICHAEL ENGH, S.J., '72 ON WOMEN COMING TO THE WESTCHESTER CAMPUS When Marymount College moved on campus, it was approximately two-thirds guys and one-third women. ... The women moving on campus certainly changed the social life at that time. Then within five or six years, there were more women than men, and it has stayed the same ever since. The old boys' school, or the boys' school with a women's college next door, became a men and women's university with women in predominance.

RENÉE HARRANGUE '57 ON NEGOTIATING THE MERGER WITH THE JESUITS The big stumbling block is what the name of this institution would be, and that's when they did not want Marymount in the name. This was LU, not LMU, so it would be all right to have Marymount of Loyola. Sister Raymunde said to me, "No Marymount, no merger!" I went back and naturally, we figured it out. ... We had to spend a lot of time saying, "This is Loyola, this is Marymount, and you all belong here."

# 1980s

PROFESSOR ARTHUR GROSS-SCHAEFFER ON BEING JEWISH AT LMU The Jewish Studies Program makes a huge statement that we want Jews to be here. ... When I was initially here [in 1980] as the Hillel rabbi, we had very few students. But last year, I had a Passover Seder of more than 100 students, so it's increasing. We're never going to be a huge number, but I think our presence has increased, and the students are starting to hear that it's a safe place for Jews to come. They'll feel welcome, and they'll feel supported.

BILLY BEAN '86 ON THE 1986 BASEBALL TEAM We had an amazing team in 1986, and that was because Tim [Layana] and I both stayed and didn't sign professionally. We both became All Americans for the second time, and we were No. 1 in the nation in Division 1 for three weeks, which was incredible. We honestly could have won the National Championship, but we had some really bad luck with weather at the College World Series that year.

# 1990s

KRISTI GONSALVES-MCCABE '93 ON SISTER PEG Really one of the most powerful things about those years was having so much contact with Sister Peg, who was just an incredible, incredible woman. She changed a lot of lives, and she meant a lot to all of us. Also, being in service to the off-campus, larger community really instilled in me a desire to incorporate service in everything that I do, whether it's passing out worship aids at Mass or tutoring kids in inner city LA.

TONY BUI '94 ON BEING A FILM STUDENT I definitely felt the magic of cinema. That definitely impacted me in a profound way that I still carry to this day, because I still search for that. It's harder to search for as you get older and work in the business. It becomes much more about the business side and the money side and things like that. Magic is something you chase after and don't always get. But when you're in film school, your only obligation is to do what you love.

# 2000s

KAREN HUTCHING '00 ON SERVICE I remember my favorite service was tutoring students at St. Columbkille, a small Catholic grade school in south Los Angeles. ... It really allowed me to see another part of Los Angeles and learn more about the issues that are very real in that neighborhood. Every time I went there, I would walk away feeling like I had been given something; I would come away with such happiness in my heart. And that was how Sister Peg was, too. She made people feel that way.

JOSÉ DE JESUS LEGASPI '74 ON LMU'S DIVERSITY The most important change is the diversity. I think [LMU] has gone through a lot in terms of the diversity. I can probably say through a qualitative approach rather than a quantitative approach that the most important years for diversity were under Father Lawton. ... His principal way of [expressing] an open mind and building upon a foundation of diversity was [by placing LMU in the] world city that Los Angeles is.

# Then & Now

*What a difference
100 years can make.*

WHAT DIFFERENCE CAN 100 YEARS MAKE? From a single building in downtown L.A. to a 142-acre campus on the Del Rey hills; small satellite libraries to the state-of-the-art William H. Hannon Library; and from lumbering computing equipment to laptops with instantaneous access, the physical changes Loyola Marymount University has incurred over the last 100 years are stark. But it's the university's internal growth that really stands out.

What once offered a handful of undergraduate degrees to 105 male students in 1911 has grown into a preeminent Catholic and nationally recognized university offering an outstanding array of undergraduate and graduate programs to tens of thousands of men and women. A place where students, faculty and community members of all religious traditions speak freely about values, ethics and God.

What started as a commitment to human rights and equality has permeated and enriched LMU's curricula and co-curricular programs and initiatives, which includes seeking out and providing educational opportunities for under-represented groups.

And what inspired the men and women of LMU to serve others in Los Angeles communities has flourished into 175,000 hours of community service a year, with expanded programs in Los Angeles and around the world. Today's students see beyond the bounds of culture and class and are eager to work for the common good.

But what may be most profound is what hasn't changed at all: a university that leads by example, educating the whole person through an environment that integrates rigorous inquiry, creative imagination, reflective engagement with society, and a commitment to shaping a more humane and just world.

Looking back, LMU has always looked forward. The following pages illustrate how our past laid ground for the present, and how each day of our centennial is setting the stage for the future.

**OPPOSITE PAGE** Junior Andres Andrieu found a way to bring LMU's past into its present with a creative photography idea. His work was exhibited outside the Department of Archives and Special Collections at the William H. Hannon Library. See more of these images that bring old, familiar scenes into today's campus at **100. lmu.edu/connected.**

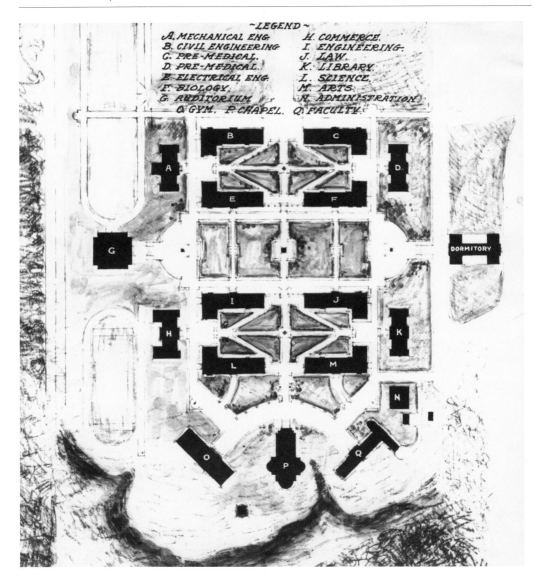

~ LEGEND ~

A. MECHANICAL ENG.    H. COMMERCE.
B. CIVIL ENGINEERING    I. ENGINEERING.
C. PRE-MEDICAL.    J. LAW.
D. PRE-MEDICAL.    K. LIBRARY.
E. ELECTRICAL ENG.    L. SCIENCE.
F. BIOLOGY.    M. ARTS.
G. AUDITORIUM    N. ADMINISTRATION
O. GYM.  P. CHAPEL.  Q. FACULTY.

The original Master Plan designed the core of the campus that is recognizable today. The 99-acre site, which was given to the university by real estate magnate Harry Culver in 1926, started with St. Robert's and Xavier Halls, which were opened for instruction in the 1929 fall semester. From Los Angeles College in 1911 Highland Park to Loyola University on the 1929 Del Rey Hills, the university has had many campus locations. View them all in an interactive slideshow at **100.lmu.edu/geography**

IMAGE BY GOOGLE EARTH

Today's campus is 142 acres, with 65 buildings and athletic facilities. The 20-year Master Plan, approved by the Los Angeles City Council in February 2011, allows the university to modernize along environmentally responsible lines. Much input from the Westchester community helped bring about the plan.

# c1930 St. Robert Bellarmine Hall

St. Robert's Hall was one of the first two buildings to go up on campus in 1929. To raise the money to build it and Xavier Hall, Father Joseph Sullivan, S.J., then president of the university, threw a major Hollywood fundraising gala, the Screen Stars Gamble. The event attracted studio heads and entertainment luminaries and is believed to have brought in as much as $300,000, mostly in pledges.

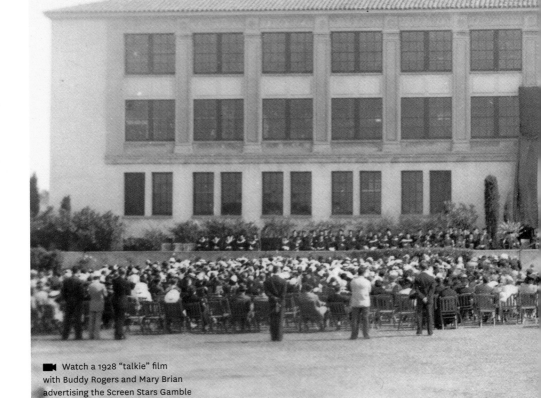

Watch a 1928 "talkie" film with Buddy Rogers and Mary Brian advertising the Screen Stars Gamble at **100.lmu.edu/livewire**

Today, St. Robert's Hall still serves as an academic and administrative building, much as it did during Loyola University's early years. In the days before cell phones and multiple electronic devices, students in a St. Rob's classroom had to rely on the hourly chimes or a view of the Bell Tower to tell the time: There are no clocks on the walls.

**LOYOLA LAW SCHOOL**, established in 1920, was among the first law schools in Southern California. During its early years, Loyola operated as a part-time evening school, and classes were taught by part-time faculty comprised of judges and practicing attorneys. In 1929, a day division was added.

In 1964, Loyola Law moved to the Pico-Union district, occupying the building that now houses the William M. Rains Library. Expansion of the law school facilities began in 1980 when Pritzker Prize-winning architect Frank O. Gehry was commissioned to design the campus. Gehry transformed the law school from one building to a full campus — designing a series of contemporary buildings clustered around a central plaza.

**TODAY**, Loyola Law School is home to prominent faculty, dedicated students and cutting-edge programs. It was the first ABA-approved law school in California to have a pro bono requirement for graduation, and LLS students donate more than 40,000 hours of pro bono work per year to nonprofit organizations.

The LLS faculty is internationally known as scholars who publish innovative theories influencing the direction of the legal profession. Yet, they are also responsive to student concerns and dedicated to their educational and professional development.

LLS graduates include trial lawyers, CEOs of Fortune 500 companies, state governors and judges. Some have become well-known and respected attorneys of the 20th and 21st centuries: Gloria Allred, Law '74, Johnnie Cochran, Law '62, Mark Geragos, Law '82, and Robert Shapiro, Law '69, to name a few.

In decades past, the best technology was large, and, by modern standards, slow to retrieve data. The uses of such equipment were limited to specialized fields and could be found only in a few classrooms.

Today, every student has access to computers much more powerful than any around in the 1960s. Every classroom is wired for optimum use and wireless access is widely available. In an animation class, the School of Film and Television puts state-of-the-art computer-aided design on every desk.

The original university library was on the first floor of St. Robert's Hall. The Charles Von Der Ahe Library opened in 1959. It comprised 42,000 square feet to house 150,000 volumes and had seating for 362 patrons in reading rooms and 12 study rooms.

The William H. Hannon Library, dedicated on Aug. 30, 2009, displays a leaf from a Gutenberg Bible and is wired to conduct real-time, interactive classes on two continents. The library uses 21st century research tools, but doesn't neglect the traditions of education built over centuries. It is the architectural centerpiece and the intellectual nucleus of the modern LMU.

## BY THE BOOK

Although this calendar leaf from a Book of Hours, in Latin, was written more than 550 years ago, it's academic value still holds strong merit for students today. This Renaissance artifact from the manuscript era is essential to teaching the very history of books and for connecting people to historical materials. Student can literally touch a piece of history.

The leaf was written on strong, resilient vellum and the natural pigments used in the ink have retained their vivid colors. Many LMU professors have their students study the manuscript leaf for its fine example of artistry and history, or they use it as inspiration for a course project. Students are able to examine and learn from the similarities and differences of old and new technologies.

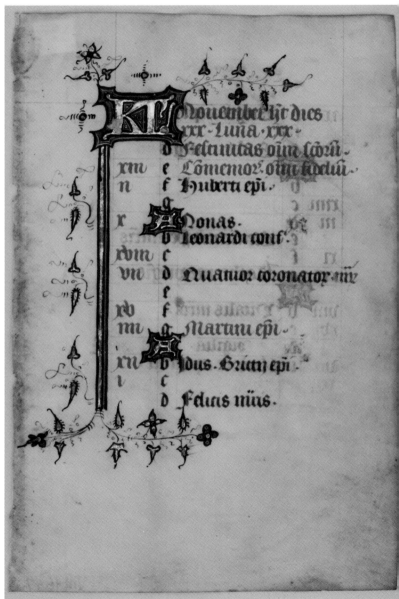

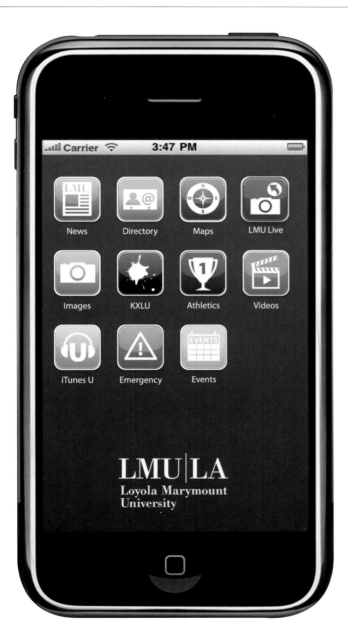

**BY THE DEVICE**

Out of the approximately 7 billion people in the world today, there are 1.9 billion Internet users and 4.8 billion active mobile users. We are living in the mobile age, and the university is responding to this phenomenon as it unfolds. Students come equipped with the latest mobile devices including smartphones, iPads and other emerging technologies, and LMU places a high importance on reaching them through these methods. However, no matter how the technology has evolved and will continue to evolve, students always come full circle and learn from the past in order to see where they will go next.

Get the iLMU mobile app and the LMU Magazine iPad app free at **mobile. lmu.edu**.

Since founding Los Angeles College in 1911, Jesuits have played an integral role in the education and formation of the university's students. Together with the Religious of the Sacred Heart of Mary and the Sisters of St. Joseph of Orange, the Jesuits have journeyed with LMU's students through their most formative years. Whether in a chapel, in a classroom or amid the beauty of LMU's campus, they have provided guidance, support and mentorship to generations of Lions.

Though fewer in number, the men and women religious on campus continue their mission to form students in the Jesuit and Marymount traditions they embody. As generations have passed, they have handed over, to dedicated lay partners, roles once reserved for religious, helping those partners become collaborators in mission. As professors, campus ministers, administrators and spiritual guides, the Jesuits and women religious continue to breathe life into the university by their very presence at and commitment to LMU.

# **1963** Mass

## SACRED MOMENTS

The celebration of the
Eucharist is at the heart of
the LMU Catholic identity.
For 100 years, the com-
munity has come together
to celebrate and pray,
to break bread and be
sent forth. Sacred Heart
Chapel has been a place
of gathering each Sunday
and on occasions of joy and
sorrow since it was built
more than five decades ago.
In 1963, Loyola University
celebrated a Requiem Mass
after the assassination of
President John F. Kennedy.
Jacqueline Kennedy wrote
President Charles Casassa,
S.J., a note expressing her
appreciation afterward.

[O] View the letter
Jacqueline Kennedy sent
Fr. Casassa at **100.lmu.
edu/jfk**

**BLESSED EVENTS** Sacred Heart Chapel was filled beyond capacity as LMU celebrated the inauguration of President David W. Burcham in 2011. With 1,100 people inside, an additional 600 participated via a video feed in the Sculpture Garden. The Mass was a fitting celebration as the university not only looked to its future under a new president but also welcomed Archbishop José Gomez to Sacred Heart Chapel for the first time. LMU has answered the Second Vatican Council's mandate of full, active and conscious participation by all, striving to create liturgies of beauty that reflect the great cultural diversity of the university and the city in which it resides.

Relive the Mass celebrating the Inauguration of President David W. Burcham at **100.lmu. edu/inaugurationmass**

# 1977 Serving Others

LMU students have long been engaged with communities in Los Angeles, working with those whose dignity is threatened. Through service organizations, clubs, social justice ministry programs and annual philanthropic events, generations of Lions worked to be women and men with and for others. Founded in 1977, Special Games has brought individuals with special needs to campus in the spring for fun, games and dancing with LMU students, alumni, faculty and staff. Four decades on, Big Day is still going strong. Watch a slideshow movie about the 2011 event at **100.lmu.edu/bigday**

Today, students complete more than 175,000 hours of service a year. The Peg Dolan, RSHM Campus Ministry Center and the Center for Service and Action have expanded their service offerings and the global reach and impact of LMU's students. CSA's Alternative Spring Breaks Program takes students to communities in Europe, Asia, Latin America and Africa, as well as domestic sites. Campus Ministry's De Colores, at 25 years, the oldest international service program on campus, makes monthly trips to Tijuana, Mexico. Additionally, students have increased their involvement in the local community, offering their time and talents to work with community partners such as Dolores Mission Church and School in Boyle Heights.

# **1968** Social Justice

**FOR 100 YEARS**, LMU has been committed to faith-driven justice. Inspired by the examples of the university's three sponsoring religious congregations — the Society of Jesus, Religious of the Sacred Heart of Mary and Sisters of St. Joseph of Orange — LMU has long worked with and for the underserved of the surrounding communities. Members of the Religious of the Sacred Heart of Mary from Marymount College and their ministries across the state showed that commitment in 1968 by standing with the farm workers of California. Maureen Murray, R.S.H.M.; Peg Dolan, R.S.H.M. '58 M.A. '74; Pauline Funk, R.S.H.M.; Joan Treacy, R.S.H.M. '67; and Catherine "Kitty" Harpur, R.S.H.M., were among the women from their community who brought bread to Cesar Chavez and Sen. Robert Kennedy as Chavez ended his 25-day Fast for Nonviolence in Delano, Calif. Today, the university honors Chavez's legacy with an annual interfaith prayer service and by observing Cesar Chavez Day as a university holiday.

**IN SEPTEMBER 2004,** when words of hate targeting ethnic and religious groups were strewn across campus hallways, students, faculty, staff and alumni marched in solidarity to show that discrimination and hate would not be tolerated at LMU. It was a testament to the university's strong commitment to fighting racial and social injustice, a commitment which began decades earlier. Following World War II, President Edward Whelan, S.J., responded to the injustice of the internment of Japanese-Americans by hiring many people returning from the camps and building apartments for them in the basement of St. Robert's Hall. Less than a decade later, President Charles Casassa, S.J., forfeited Loyola University's football game against Texas Western because LU's African-American players would not be allowed to play on a Texas field. By taking such action, LMU lives its mission to instill in students a faith that

A group of students and guests enjoyed a 1965 homecoming luau, bringing out a distinct symbol of Southern California culture: a surfboard. In 1974, the student group Na Kolea, was founded to ease the transition of Hawaiian students to Southern California. Their annual luau is now a campus tradition.

Recreation is competition for LMU's Surf Club, whose men and women take part in collegiate club contests. The club also has a service component, involved in environmental initiatives and beach-cleaning efforts. In 2009, the Surf Club was named LMU Outstanding Club Sport and earned an award for Outstanding Philanthropic Event. See a film about the LMU Surf Club at **100. lmu.edu/surf**.

STUDENT-RUN CLUBS AND ORGANIZATIONS HAVE BEEN AN IMPORTANT PART OF STUDENT LIFE AT LMU FOR 100 YEARS. Today, there are more student organizations on campus than ever before. Some of these groups stretch back to the earliest days of Los Angeles College while others are brand new to campus this year. No matter their origin, all groups play an important role in the education of the whole person. Here is a listing of many of LMU's spiritual, service, Greek, social, cultural and leisure student organizations that are part of the university's history.

**1911**
Christian Life Communities (founded as Sodality of Our Lady)

House of Philhistorians Debate Society*

Sacristans and Acolytes (founded as Sanctuary Society)

**1915**
Orchestra*

Pi Kappa Delta Speech Squad*

**1918**
Loyola Club*

**1920**
Los Angeles Loyolan (founded as A Cinder in the Public's Eye)

**1922**
The Tower Yearbook (founded as Annual; later, The Lair)

**1924**
Music Ministry (founded as the Chapel Choir)

**1929**
Crimson Circle Service Organization

**1930**
Men's Club Ice Hockey Team (disbanded in 1939; re-established in 2005)

**1931**
Del Rey Players

**1934**
Block L Society*

Pangea International Club (founded as the International Student Club)

**1935**
Loyola Marching Band*

Radio Club

Sociedad Hispania*

The Aristonians*

**1936**
Marymount Choral Club*

**1937**
Glee Club*

**1948**
Air Force Reserve Officer Training Corps Detachment 040 (Flying Lions)

**1949**
El Playano

**1952**
Alpha Delta Gamma

**1953**
Knights of Columbus*

**1954**
Phi Kappa Theta*

**1955**
Arnold Air Society

**1957**
KXLU

Student Worker Program

**1958**
Men's Club Rugby Team

**1959**
Inter-Fraternity Council*

Phi Sigma Kappa*

Resident Housing Association (founded as Resident Hall Association, reorganized in 1987)

**1960**
Belles Service Organization (founded as the Loyola Belles)

**1961**
College Democrats

College Republicans

**NA KOLEA** Twenty-five hundred miles is a long way for students to be away from home, especially when that distance is separated by the vastness of the Pacific Ocean. Each year, dozens of students travel from Hawaii to begin their life at LMU as first-year students and for nearly four decades they have made sure to bring a bit of Hawaii's distinct culture with them. Na Kolea, the Hawaiian student association on campus, was established as Hui Kumulipo in 1974 by a group of students, with assistance from John "Sam" Kileen, S.J. The current name is derived from the Hawaiian nomenclature for the Pacific Glover Bird, which winters in Hawaii and summers on the mainland. In fall 1974, the group held its first luau. The Na Kolea Luau has become an annual event hosting upward of 800 members of the LMU and Westchester communities each spring.

* No longer active

**CHRISTIAN LIFE COMMUNITIES** Christian Life Communities, or CLC, is among the largest and oldest student organizations on campus. Established at Los Angeles College in 1911 as Sodality of Our Lady, the organization has long been a part of Jesuit higher education throughout the world. Originally, it comprised students who committed themselves to communal prayer in the Ignatian tradition, attending Mass and serving the poor. It reorganized in 1968 and took the name Christian Life Communities. In the renewed CLC, participants belong to small groups who gather weekly for prayer, reflection and fellowship in the Ignatian tradition. Each group of six to 10 individuals commits itself to CLC's pillars: community, faith and service. In the past two decades, LMU's CLC program has grown to include more than 60 groups and more than 450 members, the largest chapter of CLC in the country.

**1964**
Men's Chorus*

Mount Singers (Loyola University and Mount St. Mary's College)*

**1967**
Club Football Team*

Han Tao

**1968**
Black Student Union

Gryphon Circle Service Organization

Movimiento Estudiantil Chicano de Aztlán-MEChA de LMU (founded as the United Mexican-American Students)

**1969**
Silver Wings

**1973**
Ballet Folklorico de LMU

Women's Chorus

**1974**
Hillel

Na Kolea (founded as Hui Kumulipo)

VIDA literary magazine

**1976**
Alpha Phi

Consort Singers

Panhellenic Council*

Pi Kappa Alpha*

**1977**
Asian Pacific Student Association

LMU Special Games

**1980**
Service Organization Council

**1981**
Delta Gamma

Ignatians Service Organization

**1982**
Sigma Pi*

**1985**
Men's Club Lacrosse Team

Kyodai Japanese American Club

Nikkei Student Union

**1986**
De Colores

Delta Zeta

**1987**
ROAR (founded as Lion Pride)

**1989**
Gender Sexuality Alliance (founded as Association of Gay & Lesbian Students)

**1990**
Muslim Student Association

**1991**
Concert Choir (founded as Mixed Chorus)

Kappa Delta*

Sigma Chi

**1992**
Isang Bansa

Sursum Corda Service Organization

**1993**
El Espejo

**1995**
Voices of Joy Gospel Choir

**1997**
Brothers of Consciousness

Sigma Phi Epsilon

**1998**
Feed the Hungry

Iranian, Pakistani and Sri Lankan Club

Sisters in Solidarity (founded as Sistah Friends)

Student Athlete Advisory Committee

**1999**
Armenian Student Association

Lambda Chi Alpha

Sigma Lambda Beta

**2000**
Delta Sigma Theta

Greek Council

Human Rights Coalition

Kappa Alpha Theta

* No longer active

Passion Magazine

Sigma Lambda Gamma

**2001**
LMU Pep Band

Men's Club Soccer

**2002**
Men's Club Volleyball

Pi Beta Phi

Women's Club
Volleyball

**2003**
Magis Service
Organization

Marians Service
Organization

Underwings Praxis

Women's Club Soccer

**2004**
Club Baseball Team

Harmony Unison of Beats
Dance Team

Students for Labor and
Economic Justice

The Station Bible Study

**2005**
B-Boy Status

Beta Theta Pi

Club Surf Team

Laser Squad Bravo
Improv Team

Late Night

* No longer active

ROAR Network

Unite for Sight

**2006**
Delta Delta Delta

eXaLT (founded as Petros)

Sigma Gamma Rho

**2007**
ECO Students

Latin Dance Club

Women's Club
Basketball

**2008**
Anti-Slavery Coalition

Engineers Without Borders

Lion Car Club

Melkam Akwaaba

Resilience

Shin Kanarazu Daiko

Triathlon Club

Virtuous Motion
Dance Ministry

Women's Club Water Polo

**2009**
Animation Club

Club Tennis Team

Creare Service
Organization

Lebanese Student
Association

Notetorius

One.LMU

Save Darfur

Ski and Snowboard Club

Student Veteran Organization

Teachers of Tomorrow

**2010**
Circle K International
Dance Marathon

Eco Motorsports
Racing Club

Fantastic Odyssey of Dining

Global Exchange at LMU

Habitat for Humanity

Latino Student Union

Multi-Ethnic
Student Union

Multi-Ethnic
Intercultural Exchange

Operation Smile

Run LMU

Transfer Friends

**2011**
Fraternal Values Society

Junior Youth
Empowerment

Orthodox Christian
Fellowship

P.E.A.C.E. - People for
Equality, Acceptance,
Community and
Empowerment

**LMU ICE HOCKEY**
Established in 1930 by Tom
Leib, Loyola University's
football coach, the hockey
team was originally an off-
season sport for football
players looking to stay
active. The hockey team,
however, was soon having
more success on the ice
than the football team on
the gridiron, winning several Pacific Coast League
championships. Despite its
success, the team disap-
peared by 1939.

In 2005, Chris Miller
'06, MBA '10 sought to
fulfill his goal of play-
ing college ice hockey by
re-establishing the team.
Tyler Goeckner-Zoeller '08
and Al Tipon '81 worked
with Miller to get a club
team started, and they
took to the ice that fall.
The team plays in the West
Coast Hockey Conference
of the American Collegiate
Hockey Association and
competes against USC
every year for the Cen-
tury Cup. The LMU Hockey
Team holds their centen-
nial game Oct. 27, against
USC.

<br>
Go back in time and watch<br>
the 1950 Homecoming Parade at<br>
**100.lmu.edu/1950homecoming**

# **1950** Building Champions

## ON THE FIELD

An unprecedented winning streak, national recognition and captivated fans — Loyola University's 1950 season was the program's best. Under Coach Jordan Olivar, the Lions rolled off seven straight victories and

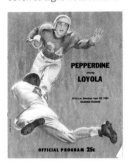

were ranked No. 20 in the nation by the Associated Press. The team was led on the field by quarterback Don Klosterman, one of the most accomplished athletes in school history.

It was a team that seemed destined for great things. Against College of the Pacific in Stockton, the Lions came from 20 points behind in bad weather to win, 35-33. Thrilling games like that caught the attention of L.A.-area sports fans. On their way to an 8-1 finish, Klosterman was one of the top passers in the nation, completing 113 of 207 passes for 1,582 yards and 19 touchdowns.

DON KLOSTERMAN earned his bachelor's degree in business administration in 1952. He was drafted by the Cleveland Browns, but was the backup to the legendary Otto Graham. Klosterman was traded to the Los Angeles Rams, but again he was playing behind future Hall of Fame quaterbacks Norm Van Brocklin and Bob Waterfield. He was playing in Canada in 1957 when he had a near-fatal skiing accident. After eight surgeries, he was told he would never walk again, but he was walking with the aid of a cane within a year. Klosterman went on to become one of the most successful professional football executives, first in the American Football League and then in the NFL.

## ON THE COURT

The Lions reached heights during the 1989–90 season they had only dreamed of before. Their stamina was strained, their system was questioned and their courage was tested.

That team averaged 122.4 points per game, still a collegiate record. The 1989–90 Lions scored more than 100 points in 12 consecutive games, tying the NCAA record, and scored more than 100 points in 28 games that season, which stands as an NCAA record.

Following the tragedy of Hank Gathers' on-court collapse during the WCC tournament and his subsequent death, the Lions riveted the nation's attention with their performance in the NCAA tournament. The team was coached by Paul Westhead and led by Gathers, Bo Kimble and Jeff Fryer.

HANK GATHERS was on his way to earning a B.A. in the College of Communication and Fine Arts — it was conferred posthumously — when he was stricken with heart failure and died at age 23. His teammates and coaches rallied after losing this much-loved player, and they continued to play at a level rarely reached before or since. His longtime friend and teammate Bo Kimble, inspired in part by Gathers' death, co-founded the nonprofit Forty-Four for Life, which works to put heart defibrillators in public places, trains as many people as it can to use the heart devices in conjunction with cardiopulmonary resuscitation, and educates people on how to maintain healthy hearts.

**ROUGH AND READY**

When Loyola University began competing in intercollegiate sports, the gear was functional and plain. Don Klosterman's football uniform from the 1950s was designed with minimal padding and protection. The football team debuted on Nov. 13, 1912, when they played a team from South Pasadena.

### TEAM SPIRIT

Modern sports gear is as much a product of a laboratory as of a field. Aerodynamically designed and ergonomically optimal, modern equipment and uniforms, like this road uniform for the LMU women's soccer team, are tailored to help athletes perform at the top of their game.

Billy Donovan '50, right, was the head Loyola University basketball coach and the leader of this 1957 kids summer camp. The university fostered a good relationship with the community and offered opportunities for local youth to compete, learn and grow during summer day camps. But the camp's origins date back much earlier than 1957. Loyola University ran off-campus summer camps at Lake Arrowhead in the '30s.

Today's summer camps are part of a robust program that continues to provide quality summer programming for the community. Each camper in each program gets encouragement and instruction in a variety of sports including tennis, volleyball, basketball, swimming, cheer, golf and several others. Fun is the goal as the camp counselors — mostly Division 1 assistant coaches and student-athletes from LMU — offer instruction and support.

Thousands of LMU students have walked through Sunken Garden for commencement over the decades. In the 1930s, the ceremonies were cozier, but no less profound. The students above shared the same joys, sense of accomplishment and, yes, some trepidation that goes with the big day.

With a show of exuberance, another class joins the ranks of LMU alumni. Because the university's reputation continues to grow, alumni will enjoy a deep sense of pride when they answer the question, "Where did you go to college?" with a heartfelt "Loyola Marymount University."

Watch a slideshow movie of the 2011 commencement class becoming alumni at **100.lmu.edu/commencement**

## LMU AT 100 CENTENNIAL YEARBOOK 2011–2012

EDITOR AND ART DIRECTOR
Maureen Pacino '93

DESIGN
DJ Stout and
Barrett Fry, Pentagram Design

EDITORIAL
Kevin Brown '08, MA '11
Margaret Butterfield '10
John Kissell
Fred Puza '09
Dena Taylor

PHOTOGRAPHY
Jon Rou
Joe August '13
Adam Garcia '11
Justin Lai '13
Nathan Podshadley '13

RESEARCH
Cynthia Becht and
Mahnaz Ghaznavi,
Department of Archives and
Special Collections, William H.
Hannon Library;
Mary Leah Plante, R.S.H.M. '64,
Religious of the Sacred Heart
of Mary Western American
Province Archives;
Neil Bethke

COPY EDITOR
Janis Rizzuto

CHAIR, CENTENNIAL
COMMUNICATIONS
COMMITTEE
John Kiralla '96

CHAIRS, CENTENNIAL
STEERING COMMITTEE
Sherrill W. Britton
Kathleen Aikenhead

Loyola Marymount University would like to thank its centennial and Rose Parade® sponsors for their generosity. Our sponsors join with us in supporting our yearlong centennial celebration as we commemorate this milestone and showcase the university's role in the history of Los Angeles and Southern California. The goal of the centennial is to celebrate LMU's past and project a clear vision of its future.

**LEGACY SPONSORS**
LMU Women's Leadership Council

OfficeMax

**HERITAGE SPONSORS**
Anonymous

Anne and Rudy F. de Leon '74

Follett Higher Education Group

William H. Hannon Foundation

Susie and Henry K. Jordan '78

Kathryn E. Nielsen '76

Joe '75, M.B.A. '79,
Carol, Brian & Erin '12 Page

Steve Page '62, J.D. '68

RICOH

Sodexo

Wells Fargo & Co.

Laura D. Williamson '74 and
Steven L. Williamson

THE CENTENNIAL YEARBOOK
WAS MADE POSSIBLE BY A
GENEROUS GIFT FROM THE LMU
WOMEN'S LEADERSHIP COUNCIL.
TO LEARN MORE ABOUT WLC,
VISIT WWW.LMU.EDU/WLC.

**COMMUNITY SPONSORS**
AT&T

Blackboard, Inc.

Timothy '82 and Michelle Dean '84

Shirley J. and Mark W. Griffin

Karen K. and Joseph M. Knott '74

Premier Vend Group, Inc.

**CENTENNIAL STEERING COMMITTEE**
Sherrill W. Britton, Co-Chair, Steering Committee

Kathleen Aikenhead, Co-Chair, Steering Committee

John Kiralla '96, Chair, Communications Committee

Cynthia Becht, Chair, Academic Affairs Committee

Jade Smith MBA '02, Chair, Student Affairs Committee

Ray Dennis MA '07, Chair, Keepsakes and Mementoes Committee

Celeste Durant, Co-Chair, Community Visibility Committee

Clarence Griffin MBA '09, Co-Chair, Community Visibility Committee

Al Koppes, O.Carm., Chair, History and Traditions Committee

Randy Roche, S.J., Mission and Ministry Office Representative

Mike Wong '89, Administration Division Representative

Kevin Brown '08, MA '11 Administrative Assistant

# Get Your 100 On!

Limited-edition gear is available at the LMU Bookstore in the Von Der Ahe Welcome Center.
310.338.2889

**Shop online: 100.lmu.edu/store**

# **2011 - 2012** Centennial Calendar

| May 6-7 | July 29 | | Aug. 30 | Sept. 7 | Sept. 8 |
|---|---|---|---|---|---|

**Unveiling of New Alma Mater at Commencement**
*Where*: Sunken Garden
*When*: Both Mornings

**Campus Celebration of the Feast of St. Ignatius Loyola**
*Where*: Sacred Heart Chapel
*When*: 11 a.m.

**The Human 100**
*Where*: Sunken Garden
*When*: 12:30 p.m.

**Pub Night: Urban Ecology with Professor Eric Strauss**
*Where*: Von der Ahe Family Suite, William H. Hannon Library
*When*: 5:30 p.m.

**Bellarmine Forum — Starting the Conversation: Where is LMU Headed?**
*Where*: Robert B. Lawton, S.J. Plaza
*When*: 12:15 p.m.

| Oct. 11-12 | | Oct. 18 | Oct. 21 | | Oct. 22 |
|---|---|---|---|---|---|

**Bellarmine Forum's Jesuit Symposium — First Annual Conference on Jesuit Higher Education: Rhetoric, Philosophy, and Theology**
*Where*: Von der Ahe Family Suite, William H. Hannon Library
*When*: All Day

**Bellarmine Forum — Jesuit Spirituality and High Finance: Can they co-exist in the 21st Century?**
*Where*: Von der Ahe Family Suite, William H. Hannon Library
*When*: 12:15 p.m.

**LMU in LA Day**
*Where*: Los Angeles City Hall
*When*: 10 a.m.

**100 Years of Service: LMU Gives Back**
*Where*: Dockweiler State Beach
*When*: 12 p.m.

| Dec. 2 | Dec. 2-4 | Dec. 7 | Jan. 2 | Jan. 15 | Jan. 18 |
|---|---|---|---|---|---|

**Men's Basketball Centennial Game vs. Columbia**
*Where*: Albert Gersten Pavilion
*When*: 7 p.m.

**Men's Basketball LMU Centennial Classic Tournament with Columbia, La Sierra, Texas and North Texas**
*Where*: Albert Gersten Pavilion
*When*: All Weekend

**Pub Night: Los Angeles' Korean American Community with Professor Nadia Kim**
*Where*: Von der Ahe Family Suite, William H. Hannon Library
*When*: 5:30 p.m.

**LMU's Centennial Float in the Tournament of Roses Parade**
*Where*: Pasadena
*When*: 9 a.m.

**Women's Swimming Centennial Meet vs. UC Davis**
*Where*: Fritz B. Burns Recreation Center
*When*: 12 p.m.

**Alumni Authors Series: Professor Kelly Younger '94**
*Where*: Von der Ahe Family Suite, William H. Hannon Library
*When*: 6 p.m.

| March 10 | March 13 | March 19 | March 21 | March 24 | March 28 |
|---|---|---|---|---|---|

**Women's Rowing vs. San Diego State**
*Where*: Jane Browne Bove Boathouse
*When*: TBD

**Softball Centennial Game vs. Notre Dame**
*Where*: Smith Field Boathouse
*When*: TBD

**Feast of St. Joseph, Husband of Mary: The Sisters of St. Joseph of Orange Celebrate 100 Years as a Congregation**
*Where*: Sacred Heart Chapel
*When*: 12:15 p.m.

**Bellarmine Forum — Contemplating LMU: A Tapestry of Spiritual Traditions**
*Where*: LMU Bluff
*When*: 6 p.m.

**Centennial National Day of Service**
*Where*: Nationwide
*When*: All Day

**Alumni Authors Series: Professor Emerita Graciela Limon '58**
*Where*: Von der Ahe Family Suite, William H. Hannon Library
*When*: 6 p.m.